Psychic Protection

Books by John-Roger

Blessings of Light
The Consciousness of Soul
Divine Essence
Dream Voyages
Forgiveness – The Key to the Kingdom
Fulfilling Your Spiritual Promise
God Is Your Partner
Inner Worlds of Meditation
Journey of a Soul
Living Love from the Spiritual Heart
Loving Each Day
Loving Each Day for Moms & Dads
Loving Each Day for Peacemakers
Manual on Using the Light
Momentum: Letting Love Lead (with Paul Kaye)
Passage Into Spirit
The Path to Mastership
The Power Within You
Psychic Protection
Relationships: Love, Marriage and Spirit
The Rest of Your Life (with Paul Kaye)
Serving and Giving: Gateways to Higher Consciousness
(with Paul Kaye)
Sex, Spirit and You
The Spiritual Family
Spiritual High (with Michael McBay, M.D.)
The Spiritual Promise
Spiritual Warrior: The Art of Spiritual Living
The Tao of Spirit
Timeless Wisdoms
Walking with the Lord
The Way Out Book
Wealth & Higher Consciousness
What's It Like Being You? (with Paul Kaye)
When Are You Coming Home? (with Pauli Sanderson)

JOHN-ROGER

PSYCHIC PROTECTION

Revised & Expanded Edition of

Possessions, Projections, & Entities

NEW TECHNIQUES AND INFORMATION

M

Mandeville Press

Los Angeles, California

Mandeville Press
Los Angeles, California
P.O.Box 513935
Los Angeles, CA 90051-1935

Published 1976. Revised Edition 1997.

Printed in the United States of America

Library of Congress Catalog Card
Number: 99-167071

I.S.B.N. 0-914829-69-6

CONTENTS

In recent years we have seen a great upsurge of interest in certain aspects of the occult—witchcraft, black magic, satanism, obsessions, possessions, entities, and so forth. All of these aspects of the occult have levels of validity and reality in one sense of the word; when seen from the higher consciousness of pure Spirit, however, reality becomes very easy to discern from illusion. The occult is not to be feared. It cannot harm you or hurt you if you understand what it is, how to recognize it, and how to protect yourself—if needed—from its negative effects.

There are many aspects of the occult experience that take place on levels other than the conscious level.

Thus it is important, if you are to understand the occult experience, that you understand these other levels of consciousness.

Within each and every human, there are several levels of consciousness. One of these levels can be identified as the *conscious self* or the rational self,—that level which thinks in a logical, cognitive pattern, which makes decisions, and which is generally responsible for directing one's life path. The *subconscious mind* exists just below the rational mind or the conscious self. It has access to much material and memory which the conscious self has "lost." It can support and work with the conscious self. The *basic self* or *lower self* exists below the subconscious mind. It has memory of all past actions of this lifetime, controls the "involuntary" body functions, and acts as guardian and protector to the body's chakra centers (in the areas of the knees, the reproductive system, the stomach, the heart, the spleen, the liver, the throat, the third eye, and the crown of the head). Emotionally, the basic self may act and react much like a very young child. It may live just to play and have fun and may often act irresponsibly. Sometimes it can react with tears or anger to a situation that "on the surface" (on the conscious level) doesn't seem to warrant an emotional response. The basic self can give tremendous energy and support to the conscious self or it can put up blocks—through fatigue, depression, disease, scattered energy and direction, and so forth. The conscious self may find these blocks nearly impossible to overcome. It is the job of the conscious self to educate, direct, and love the basic self so that optimum cooperation can be maintained.

The *high self* resides above the conscious self and acts much like a guide or guardian. It suggests direction but does not force the conscious self to follow that direction. The high self knows a person's life destiny and those actions that will fulfill it; it usually remains neutral in all situations, however, knowing that all is right and proper in ultimate reality.

In understanding the occult experience, it is also important to know about the several realms or planes of existance within our universe. The *physical realm* is not the only one. There are other levels, and the occult also involves some of these other levels. When you know of them and understand them, you need not be frightened of them. Fear often comes from something that is unknown. When you bring understanding to an area, when you "shed light on it," it usually is no longer frightening.

Just above the physical realm is what is called the *astral realm* or the realm of imagination. The lower part of the astral real is very close to the physical; sometimes it actually "overlaps" so that you get a glimps into it. This lower part of the astral realm can frighten you; there are forms there that do not look like us. Sometimes we call it "nightmare alley" because many nighmares can occur when you have tapped into the lower astral realm. The upper part of the astral realm is the realm of much imagination. Whatever you create in your imagination can appear as "reality" in the astral realm.

Above the astral realm are several other realms: the *causal realm,* which is the realm of emotions: the *mental realm,* which exemplifies the power of the mind; and the *etheric realm,* which is equated with the unconscious level of consciousness. All these realms are part of what is called the "negative" or "lower"worlds. They are realms of illusion. In these worlds, illusions can be created and/or projected. As an analogy, it's much like an amusement park "fun house" with a maze of mirrors that can reflect funny images to you and make things appear to be somewhere they're not or make things appear in strange shapes and forms. These worlds are areas of illusion, and that's an important concept to remember when we talk about aspects of the occult.

The positive realms are the worlds of pure Spirit. These exist above the etheric realm—the *Soul Realm* and above. These are worlds above the areas of illusion and confusion and false images. In the positive realms, all things are clear and pure. We all must learn the lessons of the negative worlds, however, before we can reside in the positive worlds.

CHAPTER 1

IDENTIFYING PSYCHIC INFLUENCES

In this physical level, psychic energies are always present, just as spiritual energies are always present. These energies do not function on any type of timeline. They are just present, here and now, always, in eternity. "Time" that was present ten thousand years ago and "time" that is present now are both the same. The energies are always here and now.

When you feel psychic energies coming toward you, realize that they may or may not be related to recent events; they could come from actions far distant in terms of time, yet entirely present in terms of the psychic energy. We're talking about eternity.

You might say, "But I don't remember." Of course not. You're not being required to remember. That "veil of for-getfulness" is part of the process.

Psychic energies can, at times, reach in and attempt to manipulate your mind, your emotions, and your body—and can often be very effective in doing just that. If you go someplace not under the influence of the psychic energies, someplace positive and uplifting, those negative energies can go with you and create doubt and fear in your consciousness about that positive experience. That negativity can block you from seeking and experiencing positive direction in your life pattern. Those energies can program you to avoid people who can help you. They can bring in thoughts of, "They're bad. They're evil. They'll harm me. They're after my money. They're after my children." And so on.

When you live from your own center, being influenced by psychic energies can sound farfetched and improbable. If you get involved in psychic meetings where you are subjected to emotional influences, however, you may be surprised at the effects. People who deal in psychic energy may harangue and harass you with emotionally-laden statements. For example, they may tell you someone or some group is evil, bad, and wicked, and you'll be ready to go hunt them down. Something inside of you really shakes and you find yourself caught up in the group energy, thinking, "They're right!"

Years ago when the Watts riots took place in Los Angeles, this process was taking place. The psychic energy was loose, and it was manipulating people in unbelievable ways. People who would probably never behave violently within their own life expression were rioting, fighting and looting. A psychic energy was taking over, and it ran its course. This only explains what was going on; it does not excuse the action.

I once traveled through an area in Boston where there had recently been some riots. I could feel where people had been fighting, where the energy was close to the energy that kills. The energy of the violence was palpable. Yet physically it was a beautiful, clear, brisk day. Part of my job, when I become aware of these "psychic attacks, " is to clear that energy, to alter, transmute or change it from the heavy influence of negativity to the positive influence of spiritual energy. It can be changed. It means recognizing the nature of the psychic attack, maintaining the integrity of your behavior in spite of the psychic energies and then bringing the spiritual essence into that space.

People get caught up in the influence of psychic energies because of something within them that seeks for power or seeks to be recognized as "God." It is that assertiveness for the individual power that can cause people to fall out of grace and leave them open for the psychic powers to attack. The attack comes to that area which is weakest, most vulnerable, most open to influence.

The sexual area, perhaps more than other areas, is one that is very open to the manipulation of psychic energies, because the sexual energy is, of itself, so intense that is creates a ready channel for psychic power to enter. In this sense, the symbology of the Adam and Eve story has great validity. Adam and Eve walked naked among themselves, and in their own purity, they did not need clothing. Yet when the psychic power, the negative energies, entered into their expression, the sexual areas were corrupted, and they covered themselves. When the psychic power comes in with the sexual power, that energy can become like an entity form, and the process becomes obsessive and destructive. In societies where there has been excessive sexual activity (in the sense of promiscuity or prostitution, rather than in the sense of love), the society is destroyed not through the sexual activity itself, but through the psychic power that manifests through the sexual activity.

People ask me if it matters if they lust after somebody. Yes, it does matter. And what you do with that lust matters more. Often the feeling you identify as lust comes into you through psychic influences, rather than through your own consciousness. You may think, "Wow! Where did that thought come from? I wasn't even interested and all of a sudden I just have to have this girl (or guy)." If that happens, it may not be your thought at all.

A lot of thoughts and psychic influences are around and it's easy to pick them up. It happens. Keep in mind that you don't have to act on every thought that comes through your mind. If lust comes in, you can get up and move out of that area. You can handle it by moving away from it as well as moving toward it.

Physical exercise will help disperse psychic energy. Running, jogging, tennis, basketball, construction, anything that uses physical energy in a dynamic, strenuous way will disperse and clear impinging psychic energies. Sitting and dwelling on things in your mind tends to compound them.

Our present prison system is an example of very poor response to the problem of psychic energies. Before being jailed, many prisoners are already greatly influenced by psychic power. In our current system, they have little, if any, chance of getting free of that influence. They sit and build up their sexual fantasies, project great energy into them, and then start projecting that energy throughout the prison. This is not necessarily a conscious process; it can be unconscious. The whole area may start experiencing difficulty and be unable to trace the cause.

If prisoners were placed into environments where they could be active and work constructively, where they could experience healthy recreational programs and active therapy programs, you would see more rehabilitation.

Many times you treat yourself as a prisoner. You fall under the influence of psychic energies and allow yourself to be held within that power. And if you place yourself in situations and environments where you can be active, work constructively or take part in healthy recreational programs, you'll see rehabilitation within your own consciousness.

There is a natural way for us to progress, and then there is the way that is attempting to control and manipulate life. We can look at this in terms of masculine and feminine polarities. The masculine attempts to control and direct his "empire;" he always strives to be in a superior position, the "macho" consciousness. The feminine doesn't have to do any of this because she is flowing in a more natural harmony with everything around, so there is no need for rules and regulations and usurpation of power.

What we need to do is blend the negative and positive polarities to come into the balance of a neutral consciousness where we can maintain and hold the power of our own self while flowing very naturally with all things around us. We take the best of both the masculine and feminine consciousness and blend them. Yes, it is ideal; and yes, it is possible.

Nature progresses in a very natural way which does not exclude the evolution of man. Some people ask, "What about the missing link?" There is no missing link. There are bridges of one race to another race to another race, and after a new race is established, there is no need for the bridge. We are in a bridging race right now on this planet. At some future point, many types of people now on the planet will be gone. There will be no sign of them; this level will be pulled away. There will be nothing to indicate that it was present; the new race will be present. Don't misunderstand—we are not dealing in time concepts of two days or two years; we are dealing in the concept of thousands and thousands of years.

Of course, records will be kept of all this, so there will be indicators of man's evolutionary progression—evolutionary in terms of going within to know all the levels with which we are involved while in the physical body. First, the physical, then the imagination, the emotions, the mind, the unconscious and the Soul. When you have established that awareness within, then you can move to the outer levels and find that the outer spiritual world directly aligns with the inner kingdom. At that point, you understand what it is all about. The understanding surpasses everything and brings with it peace and tranquility.

You may not be aware of that when you focus on the physical body, since the physical body is usually in a state of excitation. It is here to move. Individuals who sit in yogi positions until their legs become useless have violated the laws of the physical level. Many who have been called great spiritual masters have died of cancer and malnutrition because they violated the premise of the physical level, which is to know the physical level.

Branches of science like medicine, or the healing arts, are designed to know this physical body. The psychological sciences were designed to know the psyche or the Soul, although they have become more a study of the behaviors of the body. Sociology is the study of the interaction of these bodies. And psychiatrists are trying to deal with the integration of the mind, emotions, and body. That leaves those who are on a spiritual path to integrate it all from the premise of spiritual health, letting the spiritual energy flow through all the levels, bringing the total upliftment of the human consciousness.

It is really nice to be close with people who are in the physical healing arts, because things like massage and tender loving care can alleviate pain and discomfort. Sometimes going to a doctor and finding out that he cares can help you feel a lot better. just knowing that somebody cares can help you release illnesses almost immediately. It's very important to have loving care, and loving care is the spiritual action.

Every person is responsible for their total beingness. This does not mean that we don't assist one another by scratching backs or getting a friend a glass of water or giving them a ride downtown. It means we do all of these things–as long as it is part of their flow of spiritual upliftment. So perhaps sometime you don't get them the water. Instead you say, "There's the water tap and there's the glass; help yourself." That can make then feel less dependent and more secure in their own abilities and confidence level. We often do this with children so they can gain experience and increase their confidence.

Too often, when you gain a little bit of spiritual knowledge, you want to grab people and lift them up real fast. What happens when you grab them is that they trip and fall, and then they become fearful of your approach to life. Life is very natural, very simple. You make it complex by releasing energies inside of you through forms of symbology, through mentalizing and through wrong attitudes. Then a struggle goes on inside of you, and, not wanting to struggle, you push it back into the unconscious. It struggles there, and then manifests through illness or dis-ease that our present-day sciences cannot cope with. You can find yourself in a lot of physical trouble.

How do you handle this? You can practice spiritual techniques. There are many of them designed to reach into and clear levels of consciousness: meditations of various types, spiritual exercises, prayer techniques, forms of contemplation, chanting mantras and tones.[1] These techniques will focus and lift the energies; they can tie up the energies to give them form so that you can feel more confident and keep the energies flowing up in a straight line instead of waving in and out.

As you practice spiritual techniques, you become more and more familiar with the flow of energy patterns that manifest within your consciousness. As you become more familiar with the many levels of your consciousness, you feel more comfortable with yourself and with others in relation to yourself. By continually working with the energies inside of you, you learn to recognize what they are, their purpose, their function, their direction. You relax more and more with your own beingness, bringing forward a greater integration of all the levels of yourself. As this happens,

1. (For further information, see *Inner Worlds of Meditation,* by John-Roger.

you are no longer at the mercy of your physical habit patterns, emotional addictions, mental games, or unconscious urgings. You are able to successfully direct yourself into more positive patterns of behavior and expression.

You'll find when you get right down to the nitty-gritty of life, no one is going to take care of you but yourself. You are placed on the planet with everything you need already inside of you. Everything is already there. You can't be upset unless you allow it. You can't be controlled unless you allow it. You can't go crazy and lose your mind unless you allow it. You can't be possessed by a disincarnate entity unless you allow it. This puts you in a very unique position. You are a creator. You can create harmony or discord, happiness or despair, joy or depression, productiveness or lack.

You do not have to allow psychic influences to manipulate or control you.

You have a choice. You can direct your life into whatever pattern you wish. If you have been under the influence and identity of psychic energies, you can recover the spiritual identity of who you are—who you really are. When you have found that center and can maintain that center, you can assist other people from that solid base. You can demonstrate freedom, spiritual love and the Light of Spirit.

As you direct yourself from that positive place within you, you can begin to lift everyone around you into the same positive focus. You can contain and absorb the psychic influences that come into you while continuing to direct yourself in a positive way, lifting into more and more awareness of the Spirit within. It's all your choice. Spirit is always present. You need only turn toward it and open yourself to its guidance and direction, and you will be free.

CHAPTER 2

MAGIC

Magic, for the most part, involves people who want to control other people in some way or another. They "perform" magic. They create an illusion for you to get you to come along with their way of thinking, which, at the moment, may seem innocuous. Then, once you have gone along with their creation, they can turn it around and use it against you or they can threaten to do this and use your fear to control you. People in fear of magic submit and give in, which is the primary power of magic. When I talk about magic, I'm not talking about the magicians who perform on stage—most of those are sleight-of-hand artists. They are there to entertain, to show you what an illusion really is. Some of them are so fantastic that you just "know" they have to have something more happening than their dexterity.

Magic is one aspect of what is called the "occult." The occult involves esoteric teachings, and, by its very nature, means secret. It is not necessarily negative in its nature. It focuses on teaching those things that work, so that—depending on what is done with the knowledge—the techniques can be used in a positive or a negative way.

The occult teachings are secret teachings, not known to the general public because such teachings can be used in the field of black magic to control. Many teachers of the occult who are not dealing in magic talk in parables; they talk symbolically. Someone who is looking for magic will often try to "trap" them into revealing a key. Sometimes the keys are in the form of words. One of the most fantastic words going is "abracadabra." When that is placed in its proper frequency of energies and put forward in its proper form, it has an occult message that opens many secrets and mysteries. "Open sesame" is another occult term that can unlock many things. Maybe you pronounce it "open says me" because you *want* it to open and you *demand* it to open because you *must* have the key to the magic.

If you have the magic, you can then control other people so that you not only get them to do what you want, but you also get them to go away and leave you alone so you can do what you want. If I had to evaluate it, I would probably say that the greatest use of magic is getting others to go away and leave you alone. When they go away and leave you alone, you think you can go on about your way—except that the karma (cause and effect) of the planet isn't set up that way. When everyone goes away and leaves you alone, the karma keeps right on with you. To learn the karma of the planet, you must learn the occult, because that is part of it.

The occult, many times, has simple meanings to it. Let me give you an example that one of the ancient masters taught me: He said that if a burning bush can say, "I am that I am," then a Man can say, "I am that I am." This is an occult message, but people hold only to the meaning of the words and miss the esoteric, occult teachings that tell you there is much more going on.

I'm not going to explain the phrase to you. The explanation comes through the inner teachings, and as you start turning more inwardly to the wisdom that is within you, you will bypass the magic and the negative aspects of the occult and reach into the esoteric, inner teachings that are difficult to voice. Sometimes you share something very deep with someone else, and you say, "I'm not really saying it right. I don't have words for it." Those who are part of the esoteric school smile and say, "Yes, but I understand." You can look at them and know they understand. So you continue communicating on that higher level.

Those who cannot reach the wisdom of the esoteric may ask for the "magic genie" when they want something. There are magic terms, and many people use them; they certainly can be effective. But when you work in magic, you are working in the negative realms of Light, and you get everything that goes with it. I'm not saying not to do this. I am saying, know what it is so when you wish to participate you won't do it unknowingly. Then if you choose to follow that direction, You will know that you are entering into the study and the practice of magic.

Sometimes magic involves rituals. One form of magic uses voodoo rituals. For example, a voodoo ritual might require that someone take a chicken that has been "blessed" by voodoo incantations, cut the head off, and sprinkle the blood under the bed of someone who is ill; then that someone is expected to, and may indeed, get well. Can that be explained in terms of modem day scientific medicine? Probably not, but magic and voodoo do not necessarily utilize the scientific methodology which says that there must be a certain order, so that if you do "a" and "b" and "c," you'll get "d" every time. To function, the esoteric must have esoteric criteria, one of which is this: if it works for you, you use it, and if it does not work for you, you have the wit to drop

it and move to what does work for you.
This criteria lets you know that you are
studying esoteric knowledge.

The various forms of magic are not
necessarily evil things. They are dealing with certain energy levels that can
be produced from the hands and eyes
and other orifices of the body to get
people to move or be swayed in a particular way. Several years ago there was a
certain church that had become notori-
ous because of its completely unortho-
dox orientation in the occult. One day
when walking along the street, I saw the
High Priest of the church. As soon as he
saw me, he grabbed his robe and took
off around the corner like he had been
"shot out of a gun." He didn't know
who I was, but I knew who he was. I
don't know if he saw the Light Consciousness or if he saw a bolt of lighten-
ing. But had I met him, I would have sat
with him and his followers and talked to

them, all the time placing pure, positive Light with them. (This "Light" I speak of is a pure energy of great power that originates in the positive realms of Spirit.) I'd have probably upset the church, not in the sense of hurting them, but because the energy would have been shifting more into a Light consciousness, and their church had its basis in darkness.

One thing to keep in mind always is that those involved in magic and other negative forms of the occult do have a right to worship any way they want. Not that you necessarily want to worship that way—but neither do you have the right to rip down their churches. They'll fall because of their own energy patterns. You don't have to do anything except send Light and love their way; and, if they're dealing in Light and love but calling it another name, should you be offended because they don't say it your way? Heavens, no. That could be a ridiculous point of view. But you continually place out the energies of your own positive center, and from this you give to all worlds. You give from a pure love and from a feeling of oneness with all. You don't have to say, "Hey, you here are practicing black magic and you there are practicing satanism and you there are practicing voodoo—so none of you get any Light." On the contrary, God comes to the whole world, and the Movement of Spiritual Inner Awareness comes to the whole world. This Movement has not come only to one person, and because of this it will extend into greater and greater parts of the world.

MSIA has not come to say, "Join us," but to say, "May you know Love and Light and freedom and peace; may God dwell happily in your household, and may you awaken your Soul within

you so that you can know who you are
and awaken yourself and others that we
might all usher in a golden age." How
are we going to do this unless we can
bring a Light consciousness into the
dark areas of the occult? We let our Light
shine before all the world. We can walk
down the street blessing everyone who
comes our way. We can send the Light
to everyone. We see somebody and say,
"God bless you with Light and Love." If
we know they are Buddhists, we don't
add, "... and may the Christ convert
you to Christianity." We say, "Go ahead
and be a good Buddhist." God is in all
people, in all ways. If we took the word
"Christ" and completely wiped it out of
the language and added another word
like, "murmph," and if we said there's
"murmph" all over the world and may
the "murmph" be with you, we might
really stop a lot of bigotry and preju-
dice. No one would have to say, "Are

you Christian? I'm ready to fight and kill you if you're not Christian." Ready to fight and kill? How can that attitude be in those who love Christ and God? Christ came to bring love to the world. What kind of a Christian would kill in His name? This is one who practices "dark" magic, but certainly not a Christian. This is one who practices a type of "voodoo" to control others.

The areas of control, of magic, can be really subtle. There are many, many ways that one person can attempt to exert control over another. One way, believe it or not, can be prayer. People say, "Oh Lord, Aunt Susie has a cold. Oh Lord, heal her cold." The cold continues and they think, "What happened to you, Lord? Weren't you around?" But maybe it wasn't a cold; maybe it was hay fever. Maybe a better way is to ask for the Light for that person's highest good: "Lord, you know what it is. Would you assist that person in whatever way is for the highest good?"

Whenever one person enters into an area where they are attempting to control the thoughts or actions of another person, they are, in reality, practicing a form of black magic. Whenever you try to exert control over another person, that control must be returned to you. But it is important to remember that the only people who can control you are those that you allow to control you. It cannot happen unless you allow it. Do you know that anyone who can hurt you or upset you or make you angry is controlling you? If people can make you react, they can control you. It often seems that those people for whom you feel the most love and concern are those people that you allow to control you. You most often allow control from those you think you love and trust. No one else can control you because you don't give them any position to control. You can only be controlled–remember this—*if you allow it.*

CHAPTER 3

PROJECTIONS

P eople attempt to place controls on others in many, many ways. One way that is used "inadvertently" by some and completely consciously by others is thought projection. It has been shown—definitely—that people can receive the thoughts that another person projects. There have been many experiments with "ESP" that have proven this.

I've demonstrated this with groups of people time and time again. One technique I've used is to count from one to nine very rapidly and then ask everyone to think of a color—while I project the mental image of one particular color. Then I immediately count from one to nine again and ask everyone to think of a flower—while projecting the thought of one particular flower. Then I rapidly count from one to nine again and ask everyone to think of a piece of furniture—while projecting the image of a certain piece of furniture. Usually fifty to eighty percent of the people in the group "think of" the color, flower, and piece of furniture that is projected.

Another technique that I have used with groups is setting up an environment where the people present can experience seeing an individual's aura (a force field of energy surrounding the body). Then I ask the people to send negative thought patterns out to the individual, and it is very easy to observe the changes in the aura as it attempts to protect the body from the negative thought patterns. I then ask the group to send thoughts of love and Light to the individual, and all can observe the aura expand and change as it opens up to the positive, loving thoughts.

In both of these techniques, the person involved may not be aware *consciously* of the projected thought patterns; but on a subconscious and a basic self level—the person is very aware of the thought projections. The person picks them up and relays a response to the conscious self where there is some type of response—either physical, verbal, emotional, or mental.

The techniques of thought projection can be used in either a positive or a negative way. You can learn to protect yourself from negative thought projections and to project positive thoughts so that your action is clear and balanced within yourself. Spiritual law ordains that you receive what you put out. If you project negativity, you will receive negativity. If you project positive images and thoughts, you will receive positive responses. This is the law of cause and effect, the law of karma. It is a beautifully balanced law. It is also very subtle because there can be relatively large time gaps between the cause and the effect. The order of the universe is just, however, and all actions are balanced and cleared in proper timing.

Many people have watched me, in group situations, talk to a great many people and "zero in on" or pinpoint their problem areas. Some people think I'm really a fantastic clairvoyant or psychic. But it is really much more simply a matter of attention. I've paid attention to my own body so that I know very precisely what its feelings are and what it is capable of. Thus, I'm able to perceive clearly what other people are projecting without confusing their thoughts and feelings with mine; I know when they're different than mine because I keep paying attention. Most people go through many things that take them up and down and up and down. If something comes in that's down, I may say, "I know that's not part of me." So I'll look around and say, "Somebody in here isn't feeling well." I may begin to "pick up" a headache, and say, "Who's got a headache?" I know it's not my headache. You can develop this technique yourself. Then, once you have determined where a "disturbance" is coming from, you can reverse its direction and send back a thought of love, healing and balance—and you can be of great assistance to the person.

Years ago, one of my young friends came to me in a state of great concern because his parents fought with one another much of the time, and it really caused the youngster great disturbance and unhappiness. I suggested that, when his parents started fighting, he just hold a positive thought and, in his mind, keep saying, "God bless you both. I love you." So that next night his parents started fighting, and he just sat very quietly and kept repeating inwardly, "God bless you. I love You." The next day he told me what happened—his parents had stopped fighting, and a few minutes later he'd heard them laughing and kidding around in the kitchen. These techniques are powerful and they do work. If you try these, it is very important that you use a positive, loving consciousness and that you always do it *for the highest good,* not to control others or to get your way.

Probably the most effective way to project is through emotional energy. Again, this can be used either positively or negatively; it depends on your inner intent. We suggest that you do not project negativity because you are responsible to what you project. It is much nicer to project positively so a positive projection can be returned.

One of the biggest keys to this whole area of projection is the ability to focus attention. It's important. If you don't focus the attention, you're lost. Many times you need a device that helps you focus your attention. In meditation or spiritual exercises[1], I teach the use of music or mantras as focal points of attention so that the student will stop thinking and let the higher consciousness, that consciousness they are trying to contact, come forward. You're already in contact consciously with the conscious self; you're trying to get into the higher self, the spiritual self. To do this you have to remove the blocks that stand in the way.

The blocks are any negative expressions—envy, desire, jealousy, frustration, greed, avarice, and so forth. They block you from the reality of your own Spirit. They are parts of the negative self that stand in front of you and won't allow you to see the Divinity within, the God-source within. They are very effective blocks.

1. (For further information, see *Inner Worlds of Meditation,* by John-Roger.

How effective? Do you really *know* of your own divine nature? I'm not talking about assuming it or believing it or feeling it, but *knowing* it. That's how effective the negativity is that blocks you. You have a full-time job just moving through your emotional patterns. When you do become clear and balanced and positive, you can reach into the power and energy of the subconscious mind and basic self and pull that energy up to the conscious mind and on up to the high self. Then you become a Oneness in your force. But you only do this through directing your attention into each level of your own consciousness and perceiving very precisely what goes on there. In this type of work, there is no room for illusions or self deceptions.

This is one reason that spiritual work frightens some people, but there is nothing to be frightened of, because when you see yourself in absolute reality, it will be beautiful and perfect. it is only the illusions of the lower worlds that make you appear to be less than divine, less than perfect.

Too often, you may not be attentive enough to your own consciousness. You may not pay enough attention to what you feel, think, and perceive. So, not knowing your own position, you allow others to project "foreign" thoughts, feelings, and perceptions onto your consciousness. This happens often and can cause great confusion and upset. When you do this, you're letting other people run your life; you're letting other people do it for you. You might find it more comfortable to "do it for yourself." If you allow other people to take your experiences away from you, you do not gain the ability to handle your own experiences, to become responsible to yourself and others, and to gain the strength necessary to go on. Then you find that you have to come back to that experience sometime and do it again in some other situation so that you can learn it. It's easier to do it right now, in this moment, because right now you can handle it.

You're never given anything that you can't handle—right now. If you can keep that in mind, you'll move through your experiences with greater ease and confidence, and you'll have good experiences because you'll be learning. You'll have good days; you'll have good weeks. There really aren't any "bad" weeks. If you say, "I've had a down week," that's okay because that's just a description. But if you say, "I've had a 'bad' week or a 'lousy' week," you've probably projected your negative emotion out onto the experience of that week. I go through the same weeks that everybody else goes through, and I have very good weeks. I can be in the same room with people all day long, and they can sit there with their worlds really terrible, and my world can be just beautiful. It's all the same world: they've just projected their illusions out and then held onto that. They have judged what's there instead of looking at it for what is there— keeping the emotions in check and the attention f lowing from one experience to the next.

Sometimes it's hard to see things the way they really are. People say, "I'm lonely." I say, "What do you mean? Are you by yourself?"

They say, "Yes."

I say, "Then aren't you just alone? Isn't 'lonely' just your interpretation of your experience?" You'll be much further ahead if you don't project judgments onto your experiences.

One of the biggest illusions that people project onto their experiences is, "I'm depressed!" Often when people say this, I say, "Really? What does depressed look like?"

They say, "Nothing, it's a feeling." I say, "Do you feel like this most or all of the time?"

They say, "No, once in awhile."

I say, "Then it really isn't you, is it?"

They say, "No." And if it's not you, then it can't be true; it can't be real. The self that is real is happy and healthy. These other things come to you for a reason; they come so you can learn. If you ask people why they feel depressed, you're apt to get answers like: "Well, I wasn't invited out to dinner tonight; so I'm depressed" or "My buddy didn't come and pick me up and take me to the ball game; so I'm depressed" or "My boyfriend didn't carry my books to the locker; so I'm depressed" or "It's Saturday night and everybody else has a date, and I don't; so I'm depressed. " In all these instances, the people have looked at their experiences and projected a judgment into them. There is nothing intrinsically bad or harmful or hurtful about eating dinner at home or going to a ball game by yourself or carrying your own books to your locker or spending Saturday night with your family. These can all be very positive experiences. But you can "project" either a positive or negative interpretation on almost any experience. If you project a positive interpretation, you may find your life easier to handle.

To project love and Light, the pure essence of God's energy, you may want to use some emotional energy but not too much. To send love and Light, all you have to say is, "I ask the Light to go for the highest good." Then if it's going to go, it will go. And if it's not going to go, and you try to force it by projecting really hard, it may just come back at you really hard and be more than you might want to handle. It's easy, again, just to say, "For the highest good," and let it go. When you ask for the Light for yourself and your own situations, ask for the highest good also. It isn't necessary to put in the Light anything you can do yourself, bring the Light around you, bring the Light to you, but if you want a new car, meditation won't do it for you you have to go down to the lot where the cars are. You have to put yourself in the "car market." You have to direct your attention to the car. You can project a thought or an image out, but you are going to have to support that mental action with a little physical action if you are to fulfill it.

Projection, then, has both positive and negative aspects. In its negative aspect, it is commonly used by some people in an attempt to control others by placing an image in their mind or by placing an emotion out to them that will act as a type of "psychic blackmail." ("I'm going to be really depressed if you don't take me to the beach" or "If you don't marry me, life just won't be worth living.") Projection can be used in a positive way to project Light and love and peace and joy. By paying attention to your own levels of consciousness, to your own thoughts, emotions, and body, you can learn to identify your own expressions and thus be able to identify that which is projected towards you from another source. Then you can make a conscious choice as to whether or not you are going to be influenced by someone else's projection. The choice will be yours. As long as you direct your attention into clear perception of your experiences without placing out negative interpretations, you will walk through your life in freedom. The attitude is the key factor in all of these actions.

CHAPTER 4

THOUGHT FORMS

In the dimension next to the physical (which can be called the fourth dimension), thoughts are very real things—very real—and can be perceived rather rapidly by people who are attuned to this level. The patterns and forms of thoughts can be observed. The mind is very powerful in its action, and when it goes over and over one thing, it goes into a stage of fantasizing where it creates the patterns we call "thought forms."

Let me explain how thought forms are created, and then I will show you how they can backfire on you when used as a form of control. When you were very young, you started your conditioned responses in life. You were taught the "no-no's" and how to say "mama" and "dada"—without knowing what those things were. But as you gave a certain response, "Mama" played back to you a certain type of feeling to which you related in some way. You got something in return for what you did. In your twitchings and movings back and forth, you may have produced a "smile" that elicited a great response from Mama. This response fulfilled you in some way, so you tried to repeat that process.

Then when you became a little older, you learned the response of laughing and smiling. Man is a very suggestive being, accepting suggestions rather readily; this is one of the most effective ways children can learn and grow. But the majority of children have been trained with the approach of punishment—"No-no! Don't do that. Don't touch that!" So when children find that there are things that happen to them that they can't do anything about physically, they find out that they *can* do something about them mentally. They begin to realize that they can move away from this world that slaps their hands, punishes them, and does not allow them the freedom of their own expression. Maybe they find out that the two people they call "Mama" and "Dada" can punish them. So they start moving away from the things that they can't handle physically.

In a punishment situation the lower self can be very aggressive. I'm not just talking about the basic self; I'm talking also about the natural reflexes within each person. When the body experiences punishment or hurt, its response can be aggressive because it will want to protect itself. But when you, as a child, found out that even though you had this aggressive, self protective feeling, you could do nothing physically to avert the punishment, you started creating thought forms.

One example of the creation of a very powerful and very common kind of thought form is that which a young boy creates at the time of puberty. At this time in his life he starts realizing, through his body urges, that he wants to engage in a sexual relationship. And even though society has proscribed this as a "no-no," he must still fulfill this action. So in his own personal way, he fulfills this action, at the same time fantasizing in his mind the ideal situation. This fantasizing produces a thought form of intense emotion and sexuality. The sexual release is one of the most powerful releases there is, second only to the creative imagination. So when you take the sexual release and couple it with the creative imagination, you have created a tremendous vortex of force. As you create it, it goes out to a point that is your level of influence, and then it must cycle back. When it comes back, it must return to the creator. This thought form that has been created in great intensity comes back to you. it can do this because you have created an opening within your consciousness for it to lodge; it comes back into the place where it went out. This thought form then produces a reminiscence within you where you say, "Oh, yeah, I remember. . ." The body becomes stirred again, the endocrine system becomes active, and you then repeat that same sexual process, perhaps fantasizing the same thing or perhaps substituting another figure in the fantasy. This response now has more strength than the original response. The thought form is again released, goes out, cycles back, and activates the urging again. Imagine years of doing this.

The pattern of the sexual thought form can start off, believe it or not, by looking at a picture in a magazine. Or it can start out in a very innocuous way when a father or mother recognizes that their two- or three-year-old child has a "boyfriend" or a "girlfriend." The parents may tease and say, "Oh, is this your little boyfriend or little girlfriend? Is this your sweetheart? Are you going to marry him (or her) when you get older?" I am not saying this is right or wrong; I am saying that this is what goes on. So the very young child starts becoming aware of sexuality and what is attractive or not attractive in someone of the opposite sex. This goes on for years until the child is about twelve or thirteen years of age. Then, if the child is a boy, he may decide that "Suzie Smith" down the street fits the archetype that his fantasy has produced. Wanting to find out if this is really true, he decides that he had better explore the neighborhood. In this process of exploration, he may discover that Suzie Smith's bedroom is on the second floor and that to get there he must climb a tree. If he does this, he has entered into the consciousness of a voyeur (or what is more popularly known as a "peeping-tom") which almost every mother in the neighborhood is going to hate. Yet many of the mothers in the neighborhood probably helped promote this consciousness because of their own attitudes towards sexuality.

If the boy receives a fulfillment or gratification by seeing the object of his sexual desires, he can place her even closer within his sexual fantasy, and he has then produced a full-fledged thought form that can start directing his life. Because he will be in a very fluid state sexually, most of his waking moments will be directed toward reproducing these patterns. But it will get to the point where these patterns do not fulfill. They will release the sexual energies from him for a few minutes, and he will say, "Oh, my God, my mind's off sex for awhile; now maybe I can get some studies done or do something else." Before you know it this form will cycle back in on him because it now has a ready channel. This process where he is involved sexually with himself may happen four, five, six times a day—and each time, he creates a thought form that goes out and comes back in rapidly.

Women parallel this action somewhat, with some minor changes. The process can be universal. Some people may find that this is a process they like; they may find that it keeps them anchored down, however, and that they cannot lift up into a higher consciousness or a higher expression. When that happens, it's time to change it.

It can be very difficult to break up thought forms—not only does the mind play the desire patterns through the imagination, but after awhile, your nerves have come to expect this response. Physiologically your body has come to expect this response, and your endocrine system has come to demand this response. Then emotionally, you must fulfill this response.

Many times a person marries at a very young age in order to try to channel this action. In the marital relationship, there is an exchange of energy that takes place during the sexual encounter so that during the first six weeks of the marriage, there is a great physical and sexual closeness. After that, there is not as much closeness because the battery has become fully charged; from that point on, it does not have to be charged as often in the sexual relationship. When you are in your own individual sexuality, however, you are not receiving a complete fulfillment, because there is no exchange of energy taking place. It is a dissipation of energy, and you do not receive fulfillment.

Let's take the basic idea of this sexual fantasy, this thought form that has
been created, and continue. As the boy
gets a little older, he often feels he can
no longer continue the same sexual
pattern; so he finds a substitute for it.
The substitute pattern may very well
be drinking or smoking or eating or
something else. He starts another pattern as a substitute. He probably doesn't
need that first smoke, but he takes it.
At that point, he starts to create a new
thought form that's going to reassert
its energy on him and make him feel
like he doesn't have too much control
over his life. It takes a concerted ef-
fort to confront one of these habitual
thought forms and break it. It's rare
that you break it rapidly, because the
thought form has watched you have
the experience of trying and trying to
break the pattern and failing. Therefore, it's much like a little puppy dog—

it keeps scratching the door till it gets in. And a lot of times you let it in so it will quit bothering you, so it will quit the irritation. You give in and smoke that cigarette to quiet down. But thirty minutes later the nerves are uptight again, and it will be harder to confront this thing the next time and break it. It may win again and again and again. It's the same way with overeating and any patterns that reassert their energy on you and control you.

As a person continually projects negative thoughts or continually gives in to negative patterns of overindulgence in alcohol, food, drugs, or in some form of behavioral deviation, that action goes out and then comes back upon him. As it continues to do this, it becomes stronger and stronger until it can actually become an obsession within the consciousness. An obsession lodges itself between the conscious self and the basic self and blocks the free flow of communication. The basic self can no longer communicate with the conscious self, so the obsession can begin directing the conscious self. The person who is being controlled by an obsession may think, "I just have to have that drink" or "I just have to have more drugs" or "I just have to have this," "I just have to do that."

Many of the so-called "perverted" areas of sexual expression, like bestiality, exhibitionism, molestation, rape, voyeurism, etc., are the result of obsessions. The person who is expressing these patterns usually spends a great deal of time thinking about these things before he ever goes out and does anything about it. This is not the man who is walking by a window and stops to look inside; the obsessive pattern of a voyeur is more like the man who climbs a tree and sits there all night waiting.

If you have created an obsessive pattern within your consciousness (biting fingernails, drinking too much coffee, and smoking are other examples), you are held responsible for that action. You have put it in motion; you must learn to handle and clear it if you are to be free from that obsession. If you educate yourself, you can force these obsessions out. You can release them from their position between the levels of your consciousness. You must understand that because you put these patterns into your consciousness, you must be the one to clear them. just teaming about how thought forms and obsessions are created can be of great benefit. A lot of overcoming them is simply to exercise conscious direction, to keep yourself focused away from those patterns that are negative and focus toward those patterns that are positive. If you want the obsession back again, just go back into that situation that created it. It will be right back. The pattern of an obsession can be altered using the energy of Light; it can be changed. You can be free of the obsession and stay that way—if you do not go back into that negative pattern. People who have been using drugs heavily can come into the realization of the Light, change that pattern almost instantly, and walk away non-drug users—at that time. But if they go back into the same environment again, they may go right back into the drug pattern because the habitual desire of the body and the psychological dependency has already been established. (It's the same process for drinking, smoking, swearing, overeating, etc.) The second time the obsession gains control, it is even stronger than it was the first time. It is stronger because there is already a "space" in the consciousness where it can lodge itself. The next time it will be harder to dislodge. But it can be done.

The best way to get rid of an obsession is through conscious education in the Light, because the Light can go in and balance the situation. Obsessions don't have a high intellect, but they can block communication between the conscious self and the basic self so that you are no longer fulfilling your karmic destiny. You are, in essence, being controlled. Remember that no obsession can enter into your consciousness and control you unless you allow it. It can't come in unless you allow it or promote it. By your action of negativity, by your action of revenge, by your irresponsible action with drugs or alcohol, you leave yourself open for that obsession to come in and attach itself to your consciousness. That is why it's much better to stay as detached as you can within your consciousness and as neutral as possible.

Don't get overly concerned with physical situations. Don't go into other people's actions with them; you can get caught up in someone else's patterns. Many years ago I had a young friend who did not smoke marijuana but who went to many "pot parties" because his friends went. I told him about these patterns and how he could be caught up in their thought forms and obsessions—because he was entering into the physical situation where these patterns were being created. He said, "But I'll just love everyone there. I'll just take the Light and give it to all of them."

I said, "They'll take the Light and they'll take your love, and then you'll get taken."

He said, "Not if I just love them for their highest good."

I said, "Suit yourself," because he wasn't listening. He became a drug addict. He had carried a powerful Light consciousness; he played around with it, however, when he should have been exercising greater conscious control and direction. His action was similar to someone saying, "I'm not going to die until I'm a hundred years old," and then going out and lying across the railroad tracks. That's not using common sense.

You stay away from those areas. An alcoholic will tell you that one of the best ways not to drink is not to go into a bar. That's where the alcohol is. And another good way is not to go into a liquor store because it's there, also. The best way is to never put alcohol to your lips.

If you have to go through all those steps, however, you'll probably be drinking again. Stop the action way down the line by directing yourself into other areas. The consciousness must be educated so it will accept its responsibility and will direct into other, more positive areas; then it can remove the obsession and be free.

There are many, many people who are very adept at creating thought forms and sending them out. It can be done inadvertently, or it can be done very much as a conscious pattern. There is a story told, and it's verifiable through the Akashic records, of a woman who had studied in Tibet and learned this ability to create. She was a very lonely woman, so she created the thought form of a "man" that only she and the clairvoyants around her could see. She created a monk who contained all her heart's desires within his form. She created it beautifully, and it performed many companionable services for her, like telling her she looked nice—not by voice, but by looks. This went on for quite awhile, but then she found out that the thought form started getting more and more powerful. It became more like an entity form, a separate form with a will of its own, instead of a thought form. At times it would give her dirty looks, make her a little fearful, and try to get her to do things that it wanted done. It would make her go various places that it wanted to go and do things that it wanted to do. She became fearful and decided that she would get rid of this thought form. So she dismissed it, but it paid no attention to her and stayed. She had put so much energy into it that it could stand on its own, so-to-speak.

Then she became very fearful and the thought form grew stronger on her fear—because fear is also a form of creative energy. She came to the point where she had to speak to a spiritual teacher who had the ability of strong prayer. He prayed for her in the right manner—not for the entity to be destroyed, but for the woman to gain strength. As she gained strength, she was able to keep bringing her consciousness to bear on the thought form so she could block it. She reached the point where she no longer saw it, but she knew it was there because she could feel its presence. So she started ignoring the presence until the thing just disappeared from lack of energy. It had taken her about six months to build the thought form and about a year to get rid of it.

This points up some lessons to everyone. If you do ignore these things and continually refocus in another direction, you can, by channeling your energies, break them. You don't even really have to know that you are getting rid of this or that thought form. Simply by channeling your energies they will drop away. You are held responsible for the thoughts and images you hold in your mind. So if a negative thought crosses your mind, You can simply refocus in another, positive direction, and that thought form will drop away from lack of energy. It is important to hold a positive focus, a positive image in your mind.

There is a process—very similar to the one used by the woman to create the Tibetan monk—which is happening in some organizations today. These groups—"spiritual groups," "Light groups"—teach of an invisible Master or an ascended Master who works with the people on various levels. They may put out this information in their literature and in their study courses. Then the people, the students, take the information, add their own creativity and imagination to it, and start creating a "form" that is similar to the unseen Master of whom they have learned. As people do this individually, they create *individual* thought forms, which they then turn to as their guides. And because the forms

are created from their own thoughts
and desires, they play back to the people
what they want to hear.

If people in such "Light groups"
function in a group consciousness, they
can create a *group* thought form, which
feeds on the energy of the whole group
and can then begin to take the form of
an entity. Then as these people come together in meetings, all across the country,
the entity is attracted in by the energy that
they are holding in their consciousness,
and the entity grows stronger from that
energy. Very often the entity will identify
itself (because of the people's desires) as
being from a high spiritual level, when
it really comes out of the people's own
thought form energies which may not
be a high spiritual level. It will play back
all sorts of information that it has put
together, and people will follow and be
guided by what it says—and what they
are actually following is their own lack

of awareness made manifest. The energy can become so strong with such an entity that the people can no longer discern whether they are learning the teachings of the invisible Master or the entity. When this happens, it is possible for the people to disperse the entity if they stop holding meetings or asking for the guidance of the "master" and, in that way, pull the energy back so that the entity can no longer exist. But this can be difficult to do, because by the time such a process is recognized, some of the teachings have come from the entity form—so to disperse the entity would invalidate those teachings. It does become an interesting situation.

If there were, originally, a genuine invisible, unseen or ascended Master working with a group, and if the people, through lack of awareness, created a thought form-entity similar in form, the Master form would "back off" and allow people to work with that which they had created. As the original teachings became altered and distorted by those in the physical body, the Master, not being able to support the illusions, would pull his energy out of the group. Then the people would be working through their own energy and through the illusion of the entity they had created. Inevitably those groups who enter into this type of illusion will fall; but the entity can, and usually will, outlive the group—in a way similar to the thought form-entities which were placed with the pyramids in ancient Egypt and which are still in existence and still carry great energy today. An interesting sidelight is that a thought form-entity may become very instrumental in the revival of a religious form that has been an experience of the past. Since an entity can survive for many, many years, it may, at some point, bring forward the energy of the "old times" in greater focus and direction, starting the revival of the past religious form. Indeed, we must be careful with what person and with what group we become involved. We must always check the information we receive to see whether or not it works for us. This is one of the primary ways of determining the validity of information received. And of course, if the information works for you, it doesn't really matter from where it comes. And if it doesn't work for you, then it is not valid for you regardless of its origin.

One reason people are attracted to MSIA is because we teach people to channel their energies toward the Light, toward higher consciousness. Then the thought forms that were created by the habitual patterns you engaged in years ago begin breaking off. They break off so gradually that you often may not know it until you look back after a year

or so and say, "My God, look at all the
things I used to do that I've changed. I
don't even remember changing them."
Some of your thought forms, because
they are powerful, will try to reach out
and grab hold and pull you back into
them again. In this way thought forms
appear to have an intellect of their own,
and much of it is a false image. The
Bible says, "Thou shalt have no other
god before me." A thought form, in a
sense, is another "god." Often you have
placed it in that position. You've put
up an image: "I don't want people to
think I'm poor, so I'll tell people I've
got a very wealthy uncle back East that
I've never seen and that one of these
days I'm going to inherit a couple of
hundred thousand dollars. I'll tell them
I really come from royalty back somewhere on my mother's side of the family, but I can't quite remember what is
it." This type of "deception" is taking

a dishonest situation and setting it as a truth; at the same time, you are forfeiting divine aid. And once you set up the deception, you have to keep it going, you have to remember your story.

Have you ever noticed that when you tell a lie, you have to rehearse it quite a bit? But when you tell the truth, you don't have to rehearse. This is because the truth is a natural process, and you don't have to produce thought forms with it. All you have to do is be it, realize it. You have to work to produce false images, however, and then you have to keep focusing on these images to maintain them. You can't casually create false images and make them appear as thought forms; you must work to create and maintain thought forms. You create only a partial thought form when you go negative in your thought pattern and project out a negative image. So if you do place out a negative thought, place the

Light out right behind it so that when the negative thought cycles around and comes back to you, the Light will come right behind it and absolve the negativity. Otherwise, you may start creating a full-fledged thought form which may be much more difficult to dissolve.

When you send out a negative thought, you leave yourself open to receive negativity back through the same area. It's almost like you create a weakness that leaves you vulnerable to negativity. Do yourself a favor and send out positive thoughts and images.

If a negative thought does get out, send the Light to surround and dissolve it. The Light can disperse the negative thoughts just like soapsuds disperse when you blow on them; they just pop and are gone. The energy that was that negative thought is altered and transmuted and used in another manifestation.

The ability to create thought forms is already within you, so don't destroy the ability. Rather, take that ability and move it from the negative, from the lower realm of the earthly desires, and start transposing it very gradually into the positive. Almost all things have a positive and negative aspect; so you can use all your abilities in a positive way to lift yourself higher. Don't be as concerned about breaking an old habit as in creating a new, positive direction. When you "try" to break a habit, your basic self says, "Same old story that I've heard before; I won't pay any attention." So all of your good resolutions are to no avail; they are no good. You have to go very gradually. Then you can pull away from the "bad habits" that really aren't you.

As you go up, you're going to run into the Light someplace. It might be your own Light consciousness. Or you might just happen to make a whole circle and not find the Light. Then you know that there has to be a center to the circle, so you just start coming back in, making the circle smaller and smaller until it actually becomes a spiral. Then you spiral right into your own self awareness and say, "Why didn't I look here in the first place instead of looking out there at the edge of the circle?" The answer is that you may have been conditioned by many people—who felt they were right—to believe that God is only "out there" someplace. He may be out there someplace, but to get to Him you have to go within.

Often this is why you have such a hard time making prayer work; you are praying "out there," creating thought forms out there, when you have to go within to create your happiness. You see how you can use this creative ability with which you create thought forms? You create happiness and joy and a sense of well-being and Light and laughter; and as you keep focusing on these positive qualities in a form of prayer, you build them around you as a kind of armor—your aura becomes stronger. Then the negative thought forms start getting pushed out, first toward the periphery of your influence, and finally completely out of your consciousness. Then you have reinstituted a whole new consciousness of Light.

Quite a few years ago a friend of mine lived in an apartment house where the manager made it a habit to look through his apartment. He'd always tell the manager, "The same things that were there on Monday will be there on Tuesday, so you can save yourself the trip on Tuesday." But the manager kept coming up anyway. My friend knew when the manager had come into his apartment because he had clairvoyant abilities; he could sense the presence of the manager. He asked the manager again not to go into the apartment anymore and told him, "If you continue to do so, you might feel very disturbed." Then he placed a thought form over the door and "programmed" it so it would only give way to his own consciousness. The next day the manager went up to the apartment, went in, looked around, got a very funny feeling, walked out real fast, went downstairs to lie down, and thought he was having a heart attack. When my friend came home later, the manager's wife came to him and said, "We don't know what to do."

My friend said, "Tell your husband to stay out of my apartment and he'll feel better."

She said, "Come and look at him."

So he went and saw that the thought form was in the manager's aura. My friend told the manager, "I told you to stay out of there. If you want to go back in there again, this will happen again tomorrow." The manager said, "I won't go into your apartment anymore."

My friend said, "Okay, then this will release by itself." The manager had entered the apartment with the consciousness of snooping. His consciousness was one of guilt. He was trying to see what "spiritual" things were going on. He was looking physically so he missed the whole thing. Had he been looking spiritually, he wouldn't have opened the door.

Similar types of thought forms were placed within the tombs of the pharaohs in ancient Egypt. When the pharaohs were buried, retinues of people were buried with them, taken into the tomb alive and sealed up. These people didn't die gracefully; they died very ungracefully cursing, pulling their hair, damning everything. Their fear and negativity produced thought forms so intense that they remained there. Of course, the religious teachers, the priests of that time, also created some of the thought forms and placed them right by the entrance to the tomb. Then the thought forms they created could pull energy from the fear and negativity created within the tomb.

These thought forms were placed with the pharaohs' tombs to protect them. Once created, thought forms can exist for thousands of years with just a little energy. That's why they are so hard to break away. The thought forms that were placed there as protection ages ago are still there. When the tombs are opened, the thought forms move rapidly into the aura of the intruders. The results can be serious because those things still carry a lot of energy. If you ever go out on any archeological digs and come upon, for instance, an Indian grave site someplace out in the desert, don't go dig it up unless you're clairvoyant. The Indians were pretty smart; they knew about thought forms, too. If you could see the forms surrounding these old areas, you'd really be amazed. You can encapsulate thought forms in Light when you know what they are. You can take them right out of the air by putting the Light there and dissolving them. You can also use the Light as a protection if you become aware that people are projecting negative thoughts or control patterns against you. You can ask the Light to surround and protect you and to encapsulate and disperse any negative thoughts and images. These techniques do work, if you work them.

Daydreaming is also a method of creating thought forms. This is why I suggest that, if you must daydream, you get your daydreaming done in a hurry and get back to the reality of here and now. If you have to daydream, then bring your creativity down to this level and manifest it as creative work. Make it come "out here" in the physical so it doesn't stay in a thought form; bring it down. Make these things work for you. Otherwise they may become thought forms and try to work against you. We are on a negative realm, and the "loyal forces of the opposition" will move right into your thought form and tickle you where you live. Sometimes it's not too funny, but then sometimes all you can do is laugh because you don't want to cry in public. A grown man can look silly crying, but that can be one way to release the pain and the hurt of difficult situations.

Many people have created many things that they have to break through— not only from this lifetime, but, believe it or not, from other lifetimes, too. Some of these things are on other realms, the other realms that you're working in and through. So your work is cut out for you. Some people say, "I give up, what's the use?" But the thought form doesn't give up. If you want to come back and do it again another time, it's okay; it'll wait for you. It's in no hurry. These things can live a long, long time. That's why, when you project Light and Love, you are not only clearing yourself, but you are also clearing various other planes of consciousness. A lot of times when you say, "I love you" and "God bless you," even in your mind, people turn around and do very nice things for you. You lift them because you have helped them push some of the thought forms back from their consciousness.

As each person learns to lift himself, he becomes his own salvation. Each person then becomes his own resurrection. Jesus was a prototype. He showed us how to do it. He forgave all people, even when they had him on the Cross. He didn't produce a single thought form that would hinder or harm. He said, "Forgive them," and He let go. He didn't create any negative thought form that would wait to latch onto Him. He'll only come back to receive His good works, because that is the only work He put out.

CHAPTER 5

ELEMENTALS

There are other types of "forms" that exist which we refer to as "elementals." These exist on the astral realm and can tap into and, in some senses, communicate on the physical level. These forms have never been on the earth in a physical form; they have collected a lot of information from this realm as well as from the astral realm, however, so sometimes they can really talk a great deal with much "authority." Their "mentality," if you can call it that, is similar to a recording machine, but they can only play back information that they have heard and "recorded" at some point.

There are quite a few so-called metaphysicians and mediums whose "contacts" are elementals. These people are not necessarily aware that they are dealing with elementals because the elementals may tell them almost anything and may masquerade as highly evolved and highly spiritual beings. Then they come through and say things that are really sort of shocking, and you think, "How could a spirit that is supposed to be so highly evolved say and do those types of things? It's not logical." It is partly because of these results that this type of "spiritual" action has so often been labeled as being fake and phony—because the elementals can bring disruption and confusion and doubt to those who are unaware. Certainly some mediums do work with highly evolved contacts on the other side, but there are many who have not tapped above the elementals of the astral realm. If you have been to a medium who is working with an elemental, you'll often come away with the feeling of, "Something seems to be wrong with that" or "That doesn't seem to work" or "That didn't sound right; why would he tell me that anyway?" When those types of questions pervade your consciousness, it can be an indication that the contact may very well have been an elemental.

An elemental may come in at one moment and say, "I'm Abraham Lincoln." Once they have your attention, they may go silent and not bring forward any more information. Or the same one may come through again, this time saying, "I'm the Lord Buddha." Many years ago I was at a gathering of people who were very interested in psychic phenomena. Toward the end of the evening, they asked me if I wanted to watch as they "contacted someone." I thought the experience would be interesting, so I stayed.

They contacted an elemental who, speaking through one of the people, said his name was "Joshua." The people there were impressed, thinking it was the Joshua of Biblical times. But when I asked, "Joshua who?" it didn't have an answer. I asked other questions. I asked it which realm it lived on, if it were the astral or causal or what. It couldn't answer, which made it pretty obvious that it was a rather low astral elemental. These things are relatively easy to check out. Don't be afraid to test the Spirit, to test it constantly. Remember that you can always place the Light around something to keep out any negativity. An elemental will not and cannot harm you unless you allow it. It can only harm you if you give over your control to it and abrogate your responsibility to yourself.

One "danger" in going to a medium or clairvoyant is that an elemental can come through with some very good information that is beautiful and accurate and really works well for you. So you go back to hear more and, again, it's really fantastic. So you keep going back and back, and pretty soon you stop making your own decisions. You go to the medium and ask, "Should I change the baby's diapers tonight, or should I wait and change them tomorrow?" The elemental says, "Tomorrow will be soon enough." And pretty soon you're wondering about every little ache you have, and you run to the medium to ask what it is. Maybe you just forgot that you lifted some boxes so that you are just naturally sore. In this way the elemental can start taking away your growth and start controlling you. Elementals do not teach you how to grow and progress; they say in essence, "Come to me and don't grow." If they are not elementals, if they are spiritual teachers, they won't take your experiences from you. They'll say, "You have to go do it yourself. Here are some ways; give them a try."

Some of my students have gone through a time when they called me very often—as much as five times a day—with questions. I would often listen; I would not tell them what to do, however. As they talked, they discovered their own answers.

I can't take a person's responsibility, but an elemental will try to reach in and take a person's responsibility instantly. You can listen to an elemental; you can listen to *anyone*. If the information seems accurate and helpful, test it out. And if it works for you, use it. You don't have to get hung-up on the elemental form, however. You use the information, and then you go on. It's always important to take responsibility for your own decisions and your own actions.

Elementals can become very active when you're faced with making decisions and you're just a big mass of indecision. They'll come in and try to confuse. They will feed you information and get you to rely on them for your guidance and direction. This gives them sustenance and energy on this physical level.

If you know there are elementals around, you can educate them to the consciousness of Light. You can send them the Light, and they can be on their way. Then you can be on your way into higher expressions of consciousness.

CHAPTER 6

ENTITIES

Other disincarnate forms exist which we refer to as "entities." They are somewhat different than elementals in that most entities have been on the earth in a physical form and, for some reason, have been unable to complete their experience here. They have been "caught" or "suspended" very close to the earth and have not been able to release from this level and continue in their spiritual progression. They are earthbound. So they wait for a "body" that they can come into and possess so they can complete the interrupted action of their own life plan. They wait for someone who is not being responsible to his body; someone who is leaving his body unprotected and "open" to whatever comes in. In such a situation, an entity will often come in and attempt to take over the direction of that life. An entity possession lodges itself and creates a block between the high self and the conscious self. A possession is not necessarily bad, but it is earthbound and will block the movement of consciousness into a higher awareness.

If a person who drinks heavily dies a rather sudden, rapid, or violent death, the consciousness of that person may become earthbound because of the desire for the taste of alcohol; it becomes an earthbound entity. It will stay close to the earth plane and wait for an opportunity to possess a living human body so that it may fulfill its desire for alcohol. Perhaps the entity will wait for a preacher who preaches fanatically against drinking, because that is the thing he fights against within himself. Those things that you are fighting in your consciousness are your weak spots; and the weak spot is the place to "hit." Also, the things you fight are the things to which you give energy. So the entity will hang around, waiting for a chance to come in. At some point the preacher may let down the controls a little bit, and the possession can come in and force the preacher into an alcoholic way of life. Then you'll hear about the preacher who preaches hell, fire, and brimstone on Sunday, is drunk until Friday, sobers up on Saturday, and preaches again on Sunday. The reason that something like this can happen to a preacher is that many times a preacher may be over-balanced toward Spirit. It's important to keep the consciousness balanced and fulfilled physically, emotionally, mentally, and spiritually. You can't walk away from your body; you must take care of it and do those things that are necessary for health and balance. But you don't let it control you; you control it. The ideal is for the basic self, the conscious self, and the high self to become as one, three in one—one in direction, but each one adding an integral part that is very separate and unique.

I once knew of a minister who had the power to remove entity possessions from people's consciousness. People would go to his church services, and he would remove their entities. They thought he was the greatest person that ever existed. But months later the same people had become very disgruntled, and I could see that they had three or four new entities where there had been only one. They kept going back, and this process kept repeating itself until his group was loaded down with entities. Then the power started backing up on him and about every three to four months he would end up in the hospital for a month, trying to recuperate. He became a case of chronic walking pneumonia. He had not really been creating a positive action. He could have been educating his people about how these entities were coming in, and what allowed them in, and what to do about it—so that they could have been working with themselves consciously to remove these entities. He could have been supplying the "battery," the Light force, the strength of consciousness for his people. Then they could have pushed the entities off and regained control of their levels of consciousness, and they would have been free.

In social drinking, you are giving over your control and leaving yourself open for an entity to come into your consciousness. As soon as you feel the effects of alcohol in your system, you are no longer in total conscious control, and you leave yourself open. Many times these things come in temporarily because it is difficult for them to get hold of you if your consciousness is strong. But if you continue drinking and create a pattern of this expression by getting drunk over and over, the entities can come in a little more strongly each time, until they possess the consciousness. Once they get a hold, they can be hard to get off.

If you smoke pot or take acid trips or use any type of drugs to get high to the point that you're no longer consciously in control of your body, an entity can get on your life stream and come right in. One drug "trip" may or may not cause this. For some people, four trips may do it; for others it might take fifty. Some people try drugs once and end up in a psychiatric ward. The consciousness of every person is different. Some have stronger conscious direction than others; some have basic selves that are not very strong and cannot maintain through the experience of drugs. These people will be more susceptible to an entity coming into the consciousness. But that potential is definitely present for anyone who abuses drugs—and once that entity has come in and possessed the consciousness, getting rid of it can be extremely difficult.

Years ago I had a young friend who was a sophomore in high school, but he was certainly not one of the brightest sophomores in high school. In fact, he had a very hard time reading anything. Socially, he was a con artist. He was also one of the big campus pushers for psychedelic drugs—pot, pills, etc. He'd try anything. Once his friends told him to sniff some stuff, and it sent him on a trip—it was only a vapor decongestant. It cleared up his sinuses, too—and he thought that was a pretty good trip. But one day he came to me as I was walking down the street and said, "*Come here,* I've got to talk to you."

I said, "I'm not talking to you."

He said, "Why not?"

I said, "Because when you say, 'come here,' I don't come. I'm not your dog." He said, "But I've got to talk to you or I'll flip out."

I said, "Flip out if you want."

He said, "But this is important, I'm scared."

I said, "Good. Now, if you really want to talk to me, I'll be back here in five minutes." When I came back, he was waiting. He said, "I'm scared to death."

I said, "No you're not, or you would be dead." It was necessary to hold him to every point because this boy's perspective of life was so overly tolerant that if a bomb blew up right in front of him, he'd say, "Don't get excited; there are always other places." While the rest of the people would be pulling their hair out he wouldn't even be excited. But I had told him for many months not to go on acid trips. He was told, "I wouldn't do this; this is not for you. You are going to get possessed." Well, he thought this was one of the biggest stories he'd ever heard in his life, but now he had an entity possessing him. The particular action between his consciousness and the entity possession was not a karmic action, meaning that it was not necessary that it happen. In one sense, you could say that this particular entity possession was an accident. But it was allowed to happen because divine order is everywhere. The boy had gone very "far out" on acid. He had disregarded his body and his responsibility towards it. He was not taking care of his body or his mentality or his spiritual development. He was abrogating his rights to himself. He had given up his rights to his body and his body's functions. As he gave it up, he released his control of it and, in essence, gave that over to something else, to whoever or whatever wanted it. First he gave his control over to an acid tablet—then as he tripped, out of control, he felt something come into his body. He told me the feeling, and I told him, "You have an entity there."

He said, "I know it. What am I going to do now? How am I going to get rid of it?"

I said, "First of all, you have to realize that this entity is in your body because it wants your body. Apparently, you *don't* want it."

He said, "But I *do* want it."

I said, "Then why are you doing this to it? Why are you leaving yourself open? That acid blasts away the psychic center restraints so the psychic doors are thrown wide open and all the garbage around is welcome to come in because you've given up control of yourself. I'm going to tell you, my friend, just what it's all about. I'm going to tell you what you can anticipate. If you keep going the way you're going now, you can probably look forward to living about six months to a year longer. Have yourself a good time, because the way you do things you won't be around after that. The entity can dispossess you of your body. The entity that's with you has passed away out of its own physical body, and it can now possess yours. When it has possessed your body, your consciousness will just be loose out there, just hanging around. You won't be able to do anything; you won't be able to go anywhere. And that will be your hell." This he didn't want. I said, "That entity has come in and has gotten hold of you; it's in there. Sometimes an entity will hang around on the outside so you can sense it, but this one is in with you.

Every second and every moment it's going to be there, and it's not going to let up for a second." This was a little frightening and rightfully so, in every sense of the word. Sometimes when we get a little frightened, we get some understanding. The boy was listening—probably for the first time in his life. He was deciding that he'd better listen to someone, so he started getting a little more control back as he listened. Before this situation he had dismissed everybody; now he was paying some attention.

He was told that if he was going to get rid of the entity, he would have to force it out himself. He was told that if he even smoked a cigarette or drank some beer and got intoxicated—if he did *anything* at all that released him from his own conscious control—the entity would move in just a little more. He said, "You mean to say I can't even get drunk?"

I said, "You can do what you please, but you're going to be held responsible for the entire action." Well, this was a little rough, and he said, "How will smoking do it?" I said, "Smoking tends to shut down your Light energy; if you're going to get rid of this entity, you have to get Light—that pure energy—into your body."

He said, "What's going to happen?"

I said, "Let's just look at some possibilities. One is that you can throw that entity right off. But what it will do is to make you *think* that it is gone. It will let up that pressure in your body and you'll feel like it's not there. So you'll get out and get involved again with addictive or psychedelic experiences, and that's what it wants. It would like you to do that, so you'll get out away from the body; then it can move in a little bit more."

He said, "I don't want that. I want to know what to do." He really wanted me to reach in there and take it out. Then he'd go out and have some more trips and bring in the garbage and say, "Take it off."

I said, "I'm not going to remove the entity."

He said, "I know you can. I've come to you because no one else can help me.

I said. "If I were you, I'd go to a priest. I'd tell him what you've been doing. Then if that doesn't help you, I'd go to someone else and ask for help."

He said, "I'm here because you can help me."

I said, "You didn't listen when you were told the other times. I told you time and time again what was going to happen and you didn't want to pay any attention."

He said, "I'm listening now."

I said, "I'll talk to you a little bit later."

He went on to his school and came back a little later in the day and said," Hey, you know, it's not there anymore."

I said, "How'd you get it off?"

He said, "I sat and meditated and said I wanted it off."

I said, "Okay, if it's gone, that's fine."

He said, "Is it really gone?"

I said, "Do you want me to give you a license to go and do all those trips again?" Of course it wasn't gone. It was there, and it would do everything it could to totally possess him. If possible, it would take control of him completely.

Let's look at this situation from the point of view of the entity. The entity saw him giving up the body. It saw an opportunity, a chance. From that point of view it was not a negative action; the boy was allowing it to happen. He was going along with the action, saying it was okay. As soon as he said it was not okay, he started coming into greater balance with himself so that he possibly would be able to get rid of the entity.

When an entity comes in like this, it can assert a certain amount of control on a person, who starts feeling split because there is the person's own direction as well as the entity's direction. If this continues, the person will probably end up in a psychiatric ward somewhere receiving shock treatments. In checking spiritually, I've found that most youngsters who have been hospitalized or institutionalized because of psychedelic drug abuse have had entity possessions with them. The drugs blow away the restraints and then blow up the subconscious mind. The natural defense and protection of the body is shattered; the body is left open to whatever comes in.

Many of these entities have previously been in physical bodies where they were unable to finish what they came to do. Maybe they were killed suddenly and violently so that they made the transition with so little preparation that they became "caught" or stranded between worlds. Suicides often become earthbound because they do not complete their action here on the physical.

A consciousness that finds itself in this position is no longer on the physical level in physical embodiment; neither has it found its way to the astral realm, however. So it waits for a time when it can possess another physical body and complete its action.

Sometimes a consciousness, while in the physical body, develops such tremendous desire patterns or addictive patterns that, even when death occurs, it cannot release from those desires. So the consciousness "hangs around" the earth plane waiting to find a body that it can possess and through which it can continue to express.

If the boy who was being taken over by the entity were dispossessed from his body, he could become much like an entity form. He could become caught between worlds; much like you might get caught between two sides of a single piece of paper. He'd just be held there. As long as his physical body were still alive, he would have a responsibility to it, an attachment to it; and even though he could not express through it, he would have to "hang around." When that body died, he would be free of that attachment; he would probably still be earthbound, however.

People who commit suicide enter into a form much like this also. Because they have changed their natural and rightful development, they cannot move on to the next realm. They also can become earthbound—and they also may wait for a chance to possess someone so they can complete their experience here and move on.

Quite a few years ago a young friend was informed that he had an entity with him. I happened to be sitting with him when the other people informed him of this, and he turned around and looked at me flabbergasted, as if to say, "My God, that can't be true!" Then he said, "Is it true?"

I said, "Yes."

He said, "Why didn't you tell me?"

My answer was, "It wouldn't do any good to tell you, because there is nothing you can do with that information at this point." The other people involved proceeded to tell him that this entity was going to be with him for the rest of his life and removing it would destroy him because it was connected into his heart. Again he said to me, "Why didn't you tell me?"

I said, "Because, to me, that is bad news, and there is no way that entity can be removed at this point except to destroy you physically." He was really distraught. I said, "Now, look, it was your idea to come to these people for advice. I came because you asked me. It wasn't my idea for them to tell you that. I just kept you company because you asked. The reason I didn't tell you these things is because I didn't want to be the one who would bring this news to you. There is nothing I can do: I can't remove it."

He said, "But I know you can remove it."

I said, "Then you'd die."

He said, "I don't want to die."

I said, "Well, let's go someplace where we can sit down and talk about it."

We left and went to a quiet place, and I noticed that he was chalky white and had broken out in a cold sweat. We talked for awhile, and it was explained to him how the entity often left his body, taking his energy with it. Because it was connected to the heart, it had a "life-line" out and could be floating around anywhere while the body just dragged around with no energy. (That doesn't mean that everyone who "drags around" or who gets a little tired from a hard day's work has an entity. There are a lot of normal reasons for normal fatigue levels.)

Finally he said, "I haven't asked you the one question I guess I should ask you. What would you do if you had this?"

I said, "If I had that and knew what it was, I'd make it work for me."

He said,

"How?"

I said, "Get out your pencil and paper; here are a few suggestions. Spiritual law says you're the master of the household, and this being the case, you can command the household. Therefore you can command that entity. When it goes out, make it get information for you, and make it tell you that information when it comes back. If you want to know upcoming events or other things that are going on, command it to go (since it wants to go anyway) and to bring back, for the highest good of all, this information. And tell it that if it can't do it, it can't go."

He said, "Just like that?"

I said, "Yes, but you have to be loving and honest and sincere and appreciative and thankful. That is really necessary when you are dealing with things that are invisible."

We decided to run a rehearsal. I said, "First of all, let's get the entity to respond."

He said. "How do we do that?"

I said, "It's already responding because it's kind of interested to see what we're going to do." So I asked him what sort of information he wanted the entity to get, and he told me. Next we gave the entity the name "Harold" so we could communicate with and identify it. Then I said, "Okay, Harold you get this information for us. Now, split!"

We waited and soon my friend said, "Did it go?"

I said, "Do you have the information?"

He said, "Yes!"

I said, "Good. Write it down and wait to see if it's accurate." A few days later I called him up and asked, "What happened?"

He said, "It was accurate; it was very exact."

I said, "Don't believe it all."

He said, "Don't believe it? Why not? It was right; it worked!"

I said, "But the next time it may tell you a lie."

He said, "Oh, wow! How am I going to know the difference?"

I said, "Keep checking the information all the time to see if it works for you, and if the entity knows you are going to check all the time, then it will know that it might just as well be honest and tell you the truth. You can hold it and educate it. You've got a captive audience. You can take it to church and let it listen to some hymns and a lot of beautiful music. It may get awfully tired of fighting against your consciousness and possibly leave."

This all happened years ago, and this man has risen up through the ranks of his profession to be among the top in the nation. He has used that entity and worked with it. It has stayed with him, but it is a karmic situation that can't be released as yet. When I see him, I ask, "Well, how's Harold?" He usually says, "Couldn't be better; he's really a very likable guy and very easy to get along with. Sometimes when he rebels, I just tell him, 'Look, I'm boss!' Then he gets in line. He is even learning my profession and giving me all sorts of inspiration and hints, and I'm really coming out on top!" That's the only way to use anything that possesses you; use it to come out on top. If it's alcohol or drugs or desires or jealousy or envy that possess you, use them to come out on top. Just do that. It can be done. And you'll be further ahead.

There are people who have the ability to remove entities. It's really not too difficult, but there are some things you must consider carefully. The Bible says that if you remove one entity, more can come in its place. Let's look at this idea. It is a person's irresponsible action that allows an entity in, in the first place. Sometimes the person is aware that he is giving up control and leaving himself open. But more often, although he may be aware that his patterns and expressions are not the most advantageous, he may not be aware of all the possible consequences. So if he does pick up an entity and then goes to someone to have that entity removed, he has really not learned his responsibility for his actions and is apt to repeat the same behavior that attracted the first entity. However, the next time an entity enters, there is a "space" where the first entity was. This opening makes it even easier for the new entity, and maybe several more, to come in and attach. So by removing one entity, without educating the consciousness to protect itself, more can come in and the problem is compounded.

If people who come to work with the Light have an entity with them, we don't take it off; we educate the consciousness. We explain patterns of responsibility, and we teach people how to use the Light to direct their consciousness in a positive way. When the education really hits and lifts the consciousness, they can move the entity off by themselves. Furthermore, the entity is being educated at the same time so that when it goes, it will be able to lift into the next world and move on in its evolution. It won't go to someone else; it will be released from the earth plane.

Entities do not always come in because of drug abuse. Perhaps in some lifetime you were so very much in love with someone that you both vowed you would always be together and never be separated. Then you embodied into this time, but the other person did not. Because your vow to one another had been so strong, the other comes in as an entity—to fulfill that vow. You promised one another, and you are held responsible for that promise. Then when you pass over, you may reunite again and go on your way together—until one day you may say, "I don't think we should promise things like this anymore. Let's get rid of those promises we made four thousand years ago. We don't need that. Our love is great, but we may have separate destinies—so you go your way and I'll go my way. If we meet again sometime, fine; if not, let's just make this a good and loving parting."

One of my students who has worked within MSIA for many years had an experience similar to the one described above. She married when she was eighteen and her husband was twenty. It was during World War II. They were married only five months before he was sent overseas, and he was killed shortly after that. They had been very much in love and had vowed that they would wait for one another and be true to one another. When he was killed, he came back to her in his attempt to fulfill his promise. He hung around very close, and she was pretty aware of this. It wasn't a great disturbance to her because his presence was loving and protective, but he was "bound" to this plane and unable to move on. When she asked about it, all this was explained to her—and his consciousness was educated as well. Then they could release themselves from their binding promise and move on to fulfill their spiritual destinies.

Another way to get an entity off is through shock treatments. Psychiatrists may not know why shock treatments sometimes work, but they know they often do. An entity cannot tolerate that type of jolt, so it lets go and backs off. But it often doesn't go very far, and as soon as the body comes back into a more balanced state, it can come right back in again. This is why shock treatment is very often effective *temporarily*. But the consciousness has not been educated, and the patterns have not really been changed, so the entity usually comes back.

It is important to remember that the conscious self is "captain of the ship." It is the conscious self who is responsible for making the decisions and choosing the direction the body goes. When the conscious self makes irresponsible choices that can lead to possession by an entity, the high self will usually stand back in a neutral consciousness and allow the conscious self to learn from its actions—in whatever way is necessary for it to learn. The basic self will try to protect the body and the chakra centers, but if the conscious self persists in destructive patterns, the basic self will not be able to handle it and will probably just give up. It will not be receiving any support or positive direction from the conscious self and will eventually give up its protective function—and then the body is very open to entity possession.

We can bring these disincarnate entities into the Light; we can show them the Light. If the situation is not karmic and can be released, we call in workers from the other realms who help bridge the gap for the entities and take them into the next world. We hold them in the Light long enough so that they become educated, so that they can see that they have to assume their responsibility; then the other workers can take them into the next realm. But in the meantime, because the overall plan is so perfect, the entities have to be responsible; so they hold themselves into this orbital earthbound action until they do get this understanding, no matter how long it takes. And this is really a demonstration of love and divine order.

CHAPTER 7

PROTECTION

Whenever you work with people, it's important to keep in mind a few fundamental things about the people with whom you are working. One is that, from their physical body, they can project energy toward you in a thought pattern. Those who practice yoga have this ability. Others have developed this ability also, although not within the discipline and responsibility of yoga.

There are men who can sit in close proximity to young women and actually practice a form of psychic-sexual vampirism. They have the ability to move into a woman's psychic space and extract her body energy. Women can do this, too. This form of vampirism may not always be directed on a sexual level, and it may not always be conscious on the part of the individual doing it. There are people who can, just by being near you, pull energy from you with their own magnetic force. From your body force they can set up a magnetic attraction to get what they want from you. Unknown to you, they can be pulling you into a whirlpool pattern that will suck energy right out of you—and all you're doing is acting like a funnel for your own energy. They won't pull spiritual energy from you; if they did, it would balance them. They'll pull your body energy from you and just use it within themselves. People may sit in large groups and not know that they are "vampiring" the person next to them. We call them the "takers," and they'll take from practically anyone. The biggest takers are little babies—so you see, it's not necessarily a negative action. It's a way to get a lot of energy. Babies pull energy from adults or other, older children. They do it as a defense mechanism, to increase their own energy and to protect themselves. Teenagers are usually big "takers" too, but they do it because they are going through so many body changes and are growing so fast that they really need the extra energy.

When a person tries "vampirism" as a form of control where they are going to seduce someone in some way or another (not necessarily sexually) to get that person to do things for them, to con them, it can become a negative action. Con artists may not be so smart in their verbal expression, but they instill within you an aura of confidence. They envelop you within this magnetic force field that they are so adept at creating and they pull you right into it. Before you know it, you're thinking they're the most beautiful, wonderful people around. But if you ask for a demonstration of what they're telling you, you may find out that they're no longer around and that they've taken you for your valuables and left you holding an empty force field—the one they have placed around you. The only way that you can really counteract this action is through the art of detachment. In other words, you don't move toward a con man in the emotional body because this is where you will play the role of the "sucker"; this is where you get hit. The emotional body is where people try to take over and push you around.

There are some very good techniques that you can use to protect yourself from those people who project thought forms toward you, attempt to pull energy from you, or make any other sort of "psychic attack" against you. Your most sensitive areas are the chakra centers that are located in the torso of your body—the sexual-creative chakra, the stomach chakra, and the heart chakra. These are the areas that are important to protect when you feel negativity coming toward you. Physically you can cross your legs and fold your arms across your stomach or chest. If it's not too conspicuous, you can place a pillow or book or magazine across your stomach and hold your arms over it. Any of these things will help deflect the negativity.

Another way to protect yourself is to create, right in front of your body, a protective layer of white Light. You do this with your creative imagination. You envision white Light like cheese cloth, like a very fine mesh, and you just start building protective layers around the torso of the body. That will screen the positive from the negative, so that the negative will be caught between those layers, especially if it's a vibratory rate that you're picking up.

Then you create, in your imagination, a candle within your body in the area of the stomach center, and you envision this candle with a purple flame. You may have to work at it a little bit to see the candle and the purple flame. But once you can create that candle and flame, that purple flame will transmute any negativity coming in. Then anything negative that does get through the layers of Light will be burned up in the purple flame of transmutation. If you do this, you'll find that in situations where your stomach used to drop so that you'd feel a pulling and an energy drain, you will now feel calm and together.

Since you are learning to create as part of your destiny on this planet, you have to make sure that your creation is stabilized. For example, in the above exercise, you may need to visualize the screen and the candle there every day when you get up in the morning until you can actually see it. If you become very successful, a clairvoyant may say, "You have a white Light around your torso." These things become real as you create them. You may have to create them over and over and over as you are building strength—until you can wake up in the morning, place the Light there, place a capsule of Light around you, and have it be there. On that day, you will know that only those things that are positive will get through. If the technique doesn't work the first time, keep working with it until it does work. The choice is yours. The ability is yours.

Another way can you protect yourself is to ask for "the eight-foot cube of Light, "and it will be there for spiritual protection in the physical world. You can also just ask for "the cube of Light." This is how to protect yourself before the event occurs. To protect yourself after the event has occurred is like closing a barn door after the horse has run out. It's called dumb time. You protect yourself every time before you go out anywhere. When you go out your door, you just say, "Cube of Light." You may see it in your mind (but you don't have to see it); it's like a big box putting you in the Light. If you're going towards a large group of people, then you may say, "I want a hundred-foot Light barrier." The Spirit knows how to do this. You don't, but the Spirit does. What we do is inform the Spirit that we'd like it.

There is also a technique that you can use to clear people, places, things, etc. from yourself that you have picked up because you did not have the spiritual protection, the Light protection around you. You put the palm of one hand over your forehead and say the name of the person (or whatever, let's call it X) and then say, "Anything from or through X. Clear, disengage, disconnect." (You can also say something like "cut off," or any other verb that gets across, to you, what you'd like to take place.) Then, while your hand is still on your forehead, you ask that this be done through the Traveler, Christ, and Holy Spirit, and have the intention that it will clear completely. That's it. You might take in a deep breath or two, but you don't need to concentrate intently because whatever is going to happen is going to be done through the Spirit. After you have cleared something, immediately place the Light in and around you; then just let go of whatever it was you cleared and don't look to see if it is still there or not.

You may find that this clears whatever it is, or you may find that after about five or ten minutes or so, you feel you need to do it again, at which time you can just repeat it. Sometimes these essences clear one at a time, so you might be doing it until all of them are gone. In addition, sometimes it may take quite a few times to clear some of these things; they come off like the layers of an onion.

One other thing: when clearing a person, you may have to say the person's name backwards. In other words, say you are clearing "John Smith." You may also need to say "Smith John" when you do it, because the name has gone in "backwards."

Practice working with these techniques, and as you develop your ability and attunement to the Light, they can become as natural as breathing. As you become more diligent about keeping the Light around you, you will probably have less need of the technique for clearing yourself. All the techniques are of value, depending on your choices and needs.

CHAPTER 8

GUARDIAN
ANGELS

Since childhood you have probably heard people mention "guardian angels." But most people aren't aware that these really do exist; they are real. A lot of people may call guardian angels guides or teachers or masters. It doesn't matter what you call them because they are all doing a similar thing. They're here to assist and work with you. If you have a guardian angel with you, you can learn to contact it consciously and work with it, and it can be of great assistance to you. Very few people have more than one, or possibly two, guardian angels. Most people have only one, but some people can have two or three or four. There are some rare individuals who might have five or six, and it is even more rare if they are in contact with them. It's not rare to have a guardian angel, but it is rare to have contact with it.

Many times there is a karmic relationship between you and the one who comes forward as your guardian angel—something to be worked out between you. Also, if you have been baptized in certain faiths, there is a guardian angel placed with you at the time of baptism. Guardian angels are really there to guide, assist, and protect you.

The force field of the guardian angels that work with earthly humans is an electrical energy. One way you might feel this electrical energy, and hence the presence of your guardian angel, is through the sensation of "goose pimples" in some places on the body. You might experience tingling along an arm or leg; it's rare to feel it on the upper thigh or on the torso. Usually you feel it on the appendages: lower legs, hands, or feet. You may feel it along the side of the head, on the face, across the top of the head, or down one side of the neck. Sometimes you feel like "somebody's there." A lot of people say they feel it like a cobweb across their face; you may find yourself trying to clear your face because of this force that comes in. These experiences are all very, very interesting, especially when you have developed your awareness sufficiently to have good knowledge of who is contacting you and giving you information.

If you are going to attempt to contact your guardian angel, there are a few techniques that will probably help you to do this. The guardian angel can be contacted by going through the subconscious mind, through the basic self, and then beyond to the guardian angel. You have to learn to contact and then go beyond both the subconscious mind and the basic self. To do this, it is important to put yourself in a very relaxed, comfortable position—free from anything that will bother or distract you. As you clarify in your mind your intention of contacting your guardian angel, it is always important that you add, in your mind, "… if it is for my highest good." This protects you from "pulling in" thought forms or elementals or entities that would not be advantageous to you. Ask that the Light protect you and assist you in contacting your guardian angel.

If you sit and try to force this action, if you tighten your jaw or grit your teeth, you shut off the energy. It is through the relaxed lower jaw that you create a flow of energy that allows communication with the subconscious mind. People who grind their teeth at night may have a conflict between the subconscious and the conscious mind, often a severe conflict. So you get the jaw to relax and keep it relaxed continuously. It can be really difficult to learn to let go and relax, but to successfully contact the guardian angel, you have to become very relaxed.

One way to contact your guardian angel is to stand up with your feet comfortably apart and let your shoulders relax and slump a little so you get sort of a sway-back; as you do this, you relax the lower jaw. Remember to ask for the Light to surround you. Then you stand very relaxed and become very flexible. You then drop very deep in your consciousness and ask, "Guardian angel number one, are you with me?" It may very well just up and give you a little push. Sometimes it will push you forward a little bit. It may rock you very gently. It has to do something to make you aware of its presence. If you say, "Are you with me?" and get no response, then the guardian angel is not there. You can continue, "Guardian angel number two, are you with me?" Again, you may or may not get a response. You might ask yourself if this might not all be in your imagination. Sure, it might be. Accept all possibilities, yet try them out for size; you can test them out to see if the information you receive is accurate and helpful. If it is, does it really matter where it comes from?

I have an ancient Japanese philosopher who works with me. He has a long beard and is everything you would picture an ancient Japanese sage to be. He is my guardian angel number three. So when I want him, I say, "Okay, guardian angel number three, are you with me?" He'll let me know. I can feel him when he's with me. I also have a little German girl who works as a guardian angel with me; she's number six. She is rather clever—she hits me on the lower leg so I'll know she's there. The guardian angels can't do this unless I allow it, because I won't stand for any disturbance patterns. I communicate with them because their job is to perform certain actions. The little German girl expresses as a fourteen or fifteen year old girl, and she helps me when I am relating to young people; she acts as a go-between.

When you feel like you have made contact with your guardian angel, check it out. Ask it questions. But before you ask it questions, set up some sort of a code with it. Come to an agreement. For example, if the answer to your questions is "yes," have it push you forward and back; and if the answer is "no," have it push you side to side. Then try out a few simple questions and see if the answers come back accurately. Remember, if you stand in one position for very long—particularly if your eyes are closed—you may start rocking back and forth just as a natural balance reaction and not because the guardian angel is pushing you. So be sure you don't kid yourself; that's important.

For awhile you may not know what all the feelings and sensations mean, but as you tune more and more to the guardian angel, you'll be able to feel its hand on your head or shoulders or stomach. If you start feeling really unsure of what's happening, you might want to ask again for the Light to surround, protect and fill you for your highest good.

If you find that you have particular idiosyncrasies, you can allow for that. For instance, sometimes when people ask for the Light, they find that the Light energy starts moving their head back and forth. If this happens, you can ask your guardian angel to move your entire body when it responds, rather than just your head.

If you want to know whether your guardian angel is male or female, it will tell you. Just remember to ask it in a way that it can respond with a "yes" or "no" answer. It will give you information about how old it is, what country it's from, what racial heritage, etc. The answers might come as impressions rather than definite answers. If you continue to work with this technique, the impressions will become more and more definite. Be careful about the type of questions you ask the guardian angel, however. Don't ask questions like, "Should I go to Las Vegas next weekend?" because you are asking it to start controlling your life. But you can ask, "If I go to Las Vegas next weekend, will the trip be okay for me?" The guardian angel can answer that. You might also want to ask, "If I stay home this weekend, will that be okay for me?" If it answers "yes" to both, then the choice is yours. Don't ask, "Should I go do this or should I go do that?" because you will start pulling astral entities to you. Be careful who you contact. If you ask questions like—"Shall I put my money in IBM or in AT&T?"—you are starting to force choices. An elemental or an entity will come in and be really happy to tell you whatever it feels like telling you. Then you may start pulling in what I call "spooks." So the thing to do is always to check and double check, and always to ask for your highest good.

Sometimes when I'm busy doing things, suddenly I'll think something like, "Gee, I really should go down to Chinatown and take a look around." I'll wonder where that thought came from—so I'll check. I'll ask, "Hey, number one, are you there? Was that your idea?" If I get no response, I'll ask, "Number two, was it your idea?" If I get no response from that, I'll ask, "Number three, was it your idea?" If I get an affirmative response, I may say, "Don't go around flipping ideas at me." You have to be very "cagey" about how you check with these guardian angels, and you have to always double check. Maybe you get an impression to go downtown and do some shopping in the afternoon. Then you may want to start checking to see where this impression came from. If you've only got one guardian angel, it makes it pretty easy. If you've got quite a few it can take awhile to get through all of them.

If you ask your guardian angels a question and you start to move from side to side and then change to forward and back, you may have a big decision going. It could be a yes and no response, such as in the case of a probability. If the guardian angel with you is highly evolved, it may not give you a definite answer because it identifies universally—as a universal process, it will see all probabilities and therefore will not answer with a definite "yes" or "no."

To experience success with this technique, you may have to practice. You are, in essence, learning to talk with somebody whose language you don't know. When you are starting to communicate with these forces that are with you, you have to learn to find a language that you both can understand and use. You might have to start in sign language. Later, as you start to communicate pretty effectively, you may ask, "Is there a chance I can see what you look like?" Then the inner vision may come so that you may see that form. Then you may ask, "Can I hear your voice? Is it time for me to hear your voice?" If it indicates, "No," you can be very happy; if it says, "Yes," you can be very happy. Contacting your guardian angel takes practice.

The more you can condition your subconscious mind to release and let you go, to let you be free-flowing, the easier it is to reach to the guardian angel. If you are extremely highly evolved, of course, you can just communicate with the angels directly. But until that time, you communicate in any way that will work for you—through feeling, through images, through impressions. If you're not sure of the responses, double check. If you don't know whether or not the information you receive is accurate, stop, release it, and place the Light there again. Then ask again. If you get the same answer, and you're still not sure, let it go. Do something else. Come back to check it out later. Remember that you never, never abrogate your responsibility—the responsibility of the conscious self—to make decisions. Never give that responsibility up to an outside agent.

As you work with this technique, you'll learn more and more about it and start gaining confidence. You'll start substituting knowledge for faith. Then you take your faith and move it up a little higher; and as you gain experience, you add that to your knowledge. Then, again, you move your faith even higher. Let faith lead you, but stand upon your experience and knowledge. Get some results that are tangible to the conscious mind. That's how you build your knowledge and your confidence—through successful experiences.

If you are interested in working with this technique, work with it until you make contact with your guardian angel, until you make a good contact. Then work with it until you make an excellent contact. Work with it until you start hearing your guardian angel, talking to it, seeing it, and communicating with it just like you would with someone on the physical level. If you do practice faithfully every day, you very well may start seeing results within about thirty days. But practice every day if you want results. If you're just playing around on a curiosity level, the subconscious mind may start blocking the action—because it will run protection for these lower levels. If you're going to do this, it's important to do it in good faith. Then it can work for you.

There are many levels that are beyond the experience of the physical. These other levels and the forms that inhabit them have much reality and much illusion within them. These aspects of the occult that appear to be negative can also be very positive, depending on your intent and on your attitude. You have been given certain abilities, so you have certain potentials and certain powers. How you use these, what you do with them, is your choice.

Spiritual law says that you are held responsible for what you create and for what you express. If you want those things that are positive—peace, love, joy, and happiness—you can choose to create those things for yourself. If you express negativity and patterns of control, you will find that returned to you.

You are the master of your destiny. You can have dominion over your life plan. Use your knowledge wisely. Use your abilities wisely. Fulfill your highest potential, and you will bring to yourself freedom and joy and love.

Baruch Bashan
The Blessings Already Are

Items are audio tapes unless otherwise noted. V preceding a number denotes the tape is also available in video format. SAT stands for Soul Awareness Tapes, which are audio tapes of J-R seminars, meditations, and sharings that are sent each month only to SAT subscribers. Once you subscribe, you can obtain previously issued tapes.

Black magic, thought forms, control patterns, obsessions, and the solution

- Are You Protecting Your Weakness? (#3214)
- Creativity, Fixations, and Addictions (#7616, #V-7616)
- Does Sincerity Lead You to Spirit? (#7228, SAT tape)
- The Ectoplasmic Aura (#2108)
- Freedom from Smoking: The Freedom to Have What You Choose (Two tape album, #3802)

Black magic, thought forms, control patterns, obsessions, and the solution *(continued)*

- How to Control Thought—Aversion Therapy (#2091)
- Living in Grace, especially "Free-Form Writing" tape (Six tape album, #3903)
- Magic (#2048)
- The Masters of Destiny (#2121)
- Psychic Phenomena vs. Spirituality (#2019)
- Psychic-Sexual Energies (#3208)
- Symbology and the Unconscious (#2104)
- The Traveler & The Process of Releasing Compulsions (#3211)
- Who Gets the Karma? (#7134)

Elementals

- Working with the Devic Kingdom (#3201)

Entities
- The Hierarchy of Consciousness (#7114, SAT tape)

Guardian Angels
- The Hierarchy of Consciousness (#7114, SAT tape)

High self, conscious self, basic self
- The Three Selves (#1208)

Projection, attitude, creating, positive focus
- Are You Being Held Hostage to Your Mind? (#7351, #V-7351)
- Are Your Pictures Framing You? (#7064)
- Being Your Own Creator (#7315, SAT Tape)
- Health from the Inside Out (Four tape album, #3909)
- Hold the Image of Completion (#2613)

Projection, attitude, creating, positive focus *(continued)*

- How Can Negative Patterns Be Changed? (#2639)
- Living in a Positive Attitude (#2137)
- The Power Within You (Book, #924-6)
- A Sub-Way to Mind Control (#7079, SAT tape)
- Thoughts, Consciousness, and Manifestation (#7072)
- The Two Processes of Mind: Attitude & Altitude (#1275)
- Want to Get Free of Negativity? (#2634)
- What Are You Focusing On? (# 1132, SAT Tape)
- Who is Controlling Your Mind (#7546, #V-7546)

Protection

- Are You Living Under Law or Grace? (#7341, #V-7341)

Also included in "Living in Grace"
(Six tape album, #3903)

- Balancing Giving and Taking
  (#7274, SAT Tape)
- Discovering Courage in
  Discouragement (#7016)
- Earthquakes: Disaster vs. Blessing
  (#7519)
- Forgiveness: The Key to the Kingdom
  (Book, ISBN 0-914829-62-9)
- Forgiveness Through the Christ
  (#7185, #V-7185)
- Living in Grace, especially
  "Meditation on Forgiveness" and
  "Forgiveness Innerphasing"
  (Six tape album, #3903)
- Psychic Impunity (#7169)
- Psychic Violence (#7308, #V-7308)
- Spiritual Warrior: The Art of Spiritual
  Success (Book, available in bookstores
  everywhere, ISBN 0-914829-36-X)
- The Spiritual Warrior/El Guerrero
  Espiritual (#7333, #V-7333)
- What is Spiritual Fascism and
  Totalitarianism? (#7036)

Realms of Light
- Inner journey Through Spirit Realms (#7251)

OTHER – Ongoing Spiritual Study
- MSIA on the Internet at http://www.msia.com

The web site offers a free subscription to MSIA's daily inspirational e-mail, Loving Each Day; the *New Day Herald* online; opportunity to request that names be placed on the prayer list; MSIA's catalog, and much more.

- Soul Awareness Discourses

If you like this book, Discourses are a gold mine of further information. Here is a sample of the contents: control patterns in Discourse 11, creativity in Discourse 16; discipline in Discourses 44 and 77; elementals in Discourse 3; fixations in Discourse 52; highest good in Discourses 2 and

109; guardian angels in Discourse 131; law of cause and effect in Discourse 5, realms of Light in Discourse 3; three selves in Discourse 17; and much more. (Twelve books per year, one for each month, English, Spanish, French, Portuguese, or Italian #5000).

* Soul Awareness Tape (SAT) Series
A new John-Roger seminar every month, plus access to the entire SAT library of hundreds of meditations & seminars. (Twelve tapes per year, one sent each month, #5400)

* Dream Voyages
(Book, ISBN 0-914829-13-9)

* Manual on Using the Light
(Book, ISBN 0-914829-13-0)

* Soul Journey through Spiritual Exercises (Three tape album, with booklet; #3718)

OTHER – Ongoing Spiritual Study *(continued)*

- Spiritual Exercises: Walking with the Lord (Four tape album, #3907)
- The Path to Mastership (Book, ISBN 0-914829-16-5)
- The Power Within You (Book, ISBN 0-914829-24-6)
- The Tao of Spirit (Book, ISBN 0-914829-33-5)

Tapes and books are available from:
MSIA®
P.O. Box 513935
Los Angeles, CA 90051
323-737-4055 Fax: 313-737-5680
Email: order@msia.org
Visit our online store at:
www.msia.org

ABOUT THE AUTHOR

Since 1963, John-Roger has traveled all over the world, lecturing, teaching, and assisting people who want to create a life of greater health, happiness, peace, and prosperity and a greater awakening to the Spirit within. His humor and practical wisdom have benefited thousands and lightened many a heart.

In the course of this work, lie has given over 5,000 seminars, many of which arc televised nationally on "That Which Is." He has also written more than 35 books, including co-authering two *New York Times* best-sellers.

The common thread throughout all John-Roger's work is loving, opening to the highest good of all, and the awareness that God is abundantly present and available.

If you've enjoyed this book, you may want to explore and delve more deeply into what John-Roger has shared about this subject and other related topics. See the bibliography for a selection of study materials. For an even wider selection of study materials and more information on John-Roger's teachings through MSIA, please contact us at:

MSIA
P.O. Box 513935
Los Angeles, CA 90051-1935
(323) 737-4055 soul@msia.org
www.msia.org